The Bod

MW00720645

The Body of My Garden

Rishma Dunlop

The **Mansfield** Press

National library of Canada Cataloguing in Publication

Dunlop, Rishma, 1956 –
        The Body of my Garden/ Rishma Dunlop
Poems
ISBN 1-894469-08-9
I. Title.
PS8557.U53995b63 2002
PR9199.3.D8727B63 2002

The Publication of The Body of My Garden has been generously
supported by The Canada Council for the Arts and the
Ontario Arts Council.

Cover Design by Gabriel Caira
Text Design by Tim Hanna
Cover Photo by Barbara Cole
Author Photo courtesy of Rachel Dunlop

Mansfield Press Inc.
25 Mansfield Avenue
Toronto, Ontario, Canada M6J 2A9
Publisher Denis De Klerck
www.mansfieldpress.net

Printed in Canada

There are no gardens save those we carry within us.

OCTAVIO PAZ

the scent of you is there,
laced through the bones
of the moon

Contents

Child of Our Time

Slippage

This Tender Music

For my daughters
Cara and Rachel

Perpetual Angelus

...the dark throat which will not reject them
...the sound of the sea bell's
Perpetual angelus.

T.S. ELIOT,

"THE DRY SALVAGES," FOUR QUARTETS

Tourniquet

Language is a skin
ROLAND BARTHES

This language is tongued in water
it is so delicate, a darling,
the lip press of every syllable
lapped in sweet wells and streams

it exhales amniotic dreams,
night-birthings,
tidal pulses,
rivers of stars,
netfuls of iridescent fish,
a testament of cranes

This language is a dark siren,
your ocean throat
the voice of these hours
arpeggio of waves
speaking what we could not say,
a wet song
wrapped tight
around the unraveling heart.

The Language of Water

I am standing without you
on these city streets
in a new climate of ice and snow,
the lights on Bloor shining with promise

such absurd courage—this leavetaking
my solo-flight to the other side of the country.

Most days I am content,
my abstract longings soothed
in seductions of ivory hallways,
conversations with scholars and students,
breathing flames into my manuscripts.
I draw all this around me,
the scent of smoke in my nostrils.

But there are the hours
when I hold your name
under my tongue
until it bleeds
and memory insists on another map,
a dark and dusky knowledge,
the tawny grammar that speaks
the language of water.

And I remember a place
where the rivers empty into the bay,
the clay cliffs rising
on the edges of the Pacific Coast,
where the winds whisper secrets and
starlings fill the sky in a bolt of black silk,
where arbutus trees,
their sea-stripped limbs gleaming red
reach out for me and
the word *holy* forms in my mouth.

And I remember a time
when our bodies sang
on stormbeds
the music of wingbeats,
when you would take my hair
in your hands,
pour it down the length of my spine.

The valves of my heart
open and close
and the scent of the ocean
breaks me open
drives me to my knees.

What the Heart Knows

The heart knows your presence.
Its chambers house you,
blooded
in synapses of history.

The heart feels you
like the wind,
like the storm eye of hurricanes and gales,
a maelstrom.

The heart knows you
are figured in the drift of stars.

The heart dreams you
reads you thick like honey
spreading amber fragments of light
upon the page.

The heart stops
to hold your silence
at the still point of the turning world.

The heart tries
to grow cold
to protect itself
in the windless cold
that is the heart's heat
its ligneous musculature
braced against your name.
The heart convulses
as you throw it from
cliffs
airborne in desire,
its caverns dark
with your pulse.

The heart knows you
in its arterial arches
The dance along the artery
The circulation of the lymph
Sings below inveterate scars,
the clefts and joints
of your body
become the heart's weight.

The heart claims you.
You are sutured to
this dark organ
in permanence.

In your beginning is my end.

The heart feels you
in deliriums of fire,
the sun branding a desert sky.
It finds itself in the ashes of burnt roses,
lost gardens.
The heart burns with your heat,
gorges itself.
The sheets blaze, then turn
to salt-water.

The heart dismantles
itself
in your arms,
its valves falter
open and close.

Like *humankind*
It cannot bear very much reality.

The heart is a feathered thing,
a kingfisher's wing,
a dark dove with a flickering tongue,
releases itself,
in *the hollow rumble* of
ink-tipped wings,
plumage brilliant
in nocturnal flights.

The heart feels you in cathedrals
and churches and temples
and synagogues and mosques.
You are its prayer
By a grace of sense,
a white light still and moving,
lucid stillness.

The heart knows grief
and loss.
In your absence,
comets weep,
the heart's chambers mourn
the lights extinguished by
the empty groove in the bed
once warmed by your body.

The heart knows you have
torn it inside out,
you have rewritten
its blood-driven rhythms.

The heart *prepares for heat and silence.*
Out at sea the dawn wind
Wrinkles and slides.
In my beginning
the darkness shall be light, and the stillness the
dancing.
Whisper of running streams, and winter lightening.

The heart knows
at the still point of the turning world
you are its divided longings.
You are its fissures,
its chthonic promise,
beating steadily.

Rush Hour at Bloor Subway Station

The bodies crush
through sliding doors
adrenalin pumping
through the underground veins of the city.

I stand with them,
briefcase in hand and in this hour
I ache for those wetlands
on the Western coast
where you made me new.
I long for springtime there,
among newborn birds
nested among the reeds
preparing for flight.

I dream of you now,
of how your salt bed
changed me forever.
My tongue remembers
cutting itself
on the line of your hipbone,
the sheets of fragrant smoke,
your arms holding me against
the stormglass of the world.

In the subway station,
something rises at the edges of my vision.
An old man plays his violin,
the strings vibrating Mozart,
adagio above the steel thunder
of the approaching train.
And I smile,
my eyes suddenly flooding,
because I know

you are here with me now,
I carry your salt with me always,
you are my *white light still and moving*
my still point of the turning world,
and the night pulses hot and alive
with the beating of wings.

Terra Incognita

She moves to meet the centuries, her feet
All shod with emerald, and her light robe
Fringed with leaves singing in the jazel air.
ISABELLA VALANCY CRAWFORD, "TORONTO"

This is a city of carved stone and brick buildings, copper rooftops turned green with age, a labyrinth of subway tunnels, the steel gleam of streetcar tracks and office towers, the lights of 24 hour pharmacies. These are new maps carving themselves upon my skin. Underneath, the faint tracings of other geographies, other journeys. Your scent tangled in my sheets. And the past is a book closing in on itself. I am hoping there is room for me here, close to the harbour, on this new edge of the world. For this is a dark season. Ice demanding heat. The body remembering in the blackened wicks of winter streets. I am haunted by dreams of summer gardens, wild irises and tea roses. And it is the touch of your hands I remember, your hands on my body speaking, and in the night sky, sparks flying.

I have heard that in dark times, the eyes begin to see. If I had my way I would have you here, your body my compass. I would hold you up to the light until I could read you, your skin transparent, steeped in memory. Every scar and vein a hieroglyphic, a lover's code. Your mouth in the darkness the point where light enters me, an estuary, where the sea loosens my blood and the river runs through my heart.

City of Dreams

If love wants you, suddenly your past is
obsolete science
ANNE MICHAELS, *SKINDIVERS*

We meet in the bruised skies
of night flights
of planes and birds and angels.
We are destined for departures,
but it is too late to withdraw the heart.

Walking with you
in the blue-shadowed frost of evening
on these city streets
desire rises
in the blood-driven rhythms
of our footsteps.
The moon stretches her amber hands,
unhooking our seams.

And everywhere I look,
you are here,
in the steam pouring
from sidewalk grates,
in the steel gleam
of the #512 Streetcar on St. Clair,
in the taxis and buses,
the flower markets on Avenue Road,
in the tender flavors of sea bass and risotto
at the Italian bistro where we ate that first night.

You are a part of this city,
its skylines and stone towers,
its gargoyles and muses
and anonymous rooms.
In this embrace,
hunger is a wild thing
and the night exhales us,
your hand upon my heart.

Montréal:
Three Movements

I

L'hotel Cantlie

Bare restraint of hands on the plane. Airborne love, every touch electric. This crazy fever you and I so new to each other every cleft of skin a mystery, a gift. Winter twilight, blue-shadowed snowdrifts, windchills and lunacy, your hand on my throat in the elevator crush of mouth, the suite's French doors, windows opening to the night on Sherbrooke Street and you are there, my white shirt and pearls and lace in your teeth, the heart impossible in your hands, fierce, undone.

II

Ad Majorem Dei Gloriam

Dawn's pink finger through the white gauze of draperies. Your breathing strange and familiar. You make me coffee hot, black elixir. Your cigarette inhales the day. We walk hand in hand in the brilliance of sun. The cold air corsets me. My spine freezes. The last offering of the Montréal film festival is titled *Sentimental Destiny*. About a married man who falls in love with a woman, not his wife, their long entanglement with destiny. Too close to the bone, we decide, and choose instead to slip into Christ Church Cathedral. Light filtering through stained glass panes, angels hover, the hum of winged poems. Organ music filling us with Bach's *Praeludium*

Schmücke dich, o liebe Seele
Deck thyself, O beloved soul,

Mensch, bewein' dein Sünde gross
Man mourn for thy many sins

Passacaglia and Fugue in e minor. Sudden thaw,
my hands clasped in yours, heat rising between
my thighs, the gleam of oak pews.

III

Aurevoir

Moon over a frozen city. We laugh over wine and pasta on Crescent Street. I see you weep for the first time. It startles me. Return to the white embrace of our room. Love soft as breath, brush of fingers, this tender fragile light, taste of your skin floats on the night air, infinite. Clarity. The bed unwinds ribbons of starlight.

Grey dawn. Uncertain hour before daybreak. Damp bed of love. I watch you sleep, your measured breath the morning pulse. This is our first real goodbye. Agony we endure until we realize we will live a lifetime of farewells. Voyeurs, we watch the travelers, imagine their secret stories, as planes lift-off the runways at Dorval airport. I imagine you always flying in opposite directions, our separations of geography, history, Great Lakes, the pulls of past vows, the clamour of breakfast dishes, neighbourhoods, children. We kiss, murmur I love yous, turn away. Syllables of longing, words dissolve in my mouth. The sting of it unspoken.

The skies weep for us. Clouds and snowflakes.

The heart is buried at frequent intervals.

Aubade:
Notes to a Pilot

I hold you suspended
between breath and desire,
voiced in dusky horizons,
in the planes you fly,
in their engines'
hollow rumble of wings

I am a promise caught
between this city and yours,
our skies spanned by the white gleam of e-mail
on our computer screens
our letters leaving me hungry
for your voice
that Southern drawl
a music I have never known before,
encircling me like an amulet,
your words my talismans,
the taste of flowers
and laughter in my mouth.

In dreams I travel with you
in the deep stillness
the still point of the turning world
before your early morning journeys,
through the dark quiet hangar,
in the gleam of headlights and the instrument panel,
I am lifting your heart into flight,
cabin pressure mounting,
engines waking the world,
silver wings slicing open
the rose spill of dawn,
with the sharp blades of love.

Eros

Something brushes past my hair
catches and tangles in it.

Something grazes the optic nerve
softens the edges of darkness.

Someone is painting a gilded fresco
on the ceiling of the bell-tower.

Raven wing of hunger,
carnal winds.

The heart contracts,
systolic spasm.

The air fills with musk,
the scent of hyacinths.

Milk-spill of constellations across a night sky,
the moon bruises mauve with desire.

Your name blooms
like a cut on my mouth.

The Art of Travel: A Fable

We must have been meant for another time.
We tell each other this
as if it makes profound difference
to the story.

Once upon a time...

You imagine traveling with me
to my conferences
on trains the way they used to be,
steam locomotives,
long, sleek, luxurious.

I would have my black-veiled hat,
my gloves, my valise,
silk stockings with seams
from toe to thigh.

We would make love in a Pullman car,
dine with fine china and silver,
drink champagne from ice-buckets
in a leather- appointed berth.
We would fall asleep to the rhythmic
lullabies of engines
and your thrumming heart.

We would preserve ourselves
shining, stilled
in the glossy frame of an O. Winston Link
black and white photograph.

We know that to think too much
would disturb the heart.

We will write travelogues
of desire,
spanning continents
and the world will be brilliant
with our light.

Beloved

...You've kissed my hair
to wake me. I dreamed you were a poem

It will not be simple, it will take all your heart.
Adrienne Rich

To have loved you
is to know that
the Beloved is never
simple.

Other echoes have inhabited me.
I thought I knew my way,
the paths of entry clearly marked.
But I have known the curve
of your body
a new passage
to the rose garden,
breathing a prayer
through folds of orchids,
through river-swells of moonlight,
and love bleeds, takes flight,
snaps the stems from wildflower stalks,
opens the floodgates
of a new country,
your mouth a poem,
my book of hours,
red-lettered in mercury and sulphur,
illuminated, vellum-leafed

your silk
my private devotion
your salt skin
my tender ocean.

Prayer

Let the politician return home to his wife and infant daughter.
Let him lay his head down upon his wife's lap and let him dream.
Let him dream in blue, the color of his newborn's eyes, *tabula rasa*.

Let us hear the cries of the men and women who ache with loneliness.
Let their mouths be filled with tears and with music.
Let their solitude be the garments of angels.

Let the fearful child find an apricot, a starfish, a fistful of rubies.

Let the mothers and fathers whose children have been murdered
find boxes of moonlight.

Let the murderers lay down their weapons.
Let the taste of blood-oranges flower on their tongues.

Let the starving have the sweetness of plums.

Let lovers who have become strangers, touch each other again.
Let them feel the thrust of love.
Let it be like the first time, when skin on skin made them transparent,
coming and melting in the heat of summer.

Let the poet have her red shoes.
Let her have her liturgy of wet vowels and syllables.
Let her be the throat of these hours.

Vespers

My heart
is caught in its own traps
snares of its own making

addicted to the beauty of words
mainlining dictionaries and weather maps
I contemplate my brokenness
want the language of storms and music

I ride the kisses of zephyrs and arias
wild, symphonic gusts
I want this velocity

my art is uncertain
the tongue struggles
unhinged

reason drowns in the river's
ridged embankments
my body is water, translucent
sliding dark beneath the pool

I gulp for air
the taste of gracenotes,
ascending scales
in sea winds and tidal pools,
the dark voice of the gulf,
the sea's throat
perpetual angelus

the poem ripples to the surface,
opaline light of unknowing,
the mind's fluorescence
at the still point of the turning world,
the heart's scriptures
thawing
a soft rain, falling
falling

The Body of My Garden

words that are flowers that are fruits that are acts
OCTAVIO PAZ,
"HYMN AMONG THE RUINS"

...There, in the quiet moonlight
Is a garden, blooming red
The lotus blossoms are waiting...

FELIX MENDELSSOHN,
"ON WINGS OF SONG"

Geography

I have stitched my skirts to continents
danced on the equator
dipped my hands into the Lesser Amazon
the emerald mouths of rivers

I have opened up the Atlas with my bones
found my own wild acres

I have loved places
the azure of the Adriatic
the salt and foam of the Atlantic
the sun dissolving copper on city rooftops

but questions of travel are resolved
in these wetlands
my body an aviary
for seabirds

now I see at the edges of darkness
extremes of moonlight

in Boundary Bay
the Pacific Ocean speaks my name
reveals its voice
and water becomes my mouth

I read this place
mapped in my wet fingers
thumbing me open

Invocation

The coyote stands
in a grainy sea
the fields oceans of heat
crops sucking the air dry

I am surprised to see him
watching me at midday
I thought him a nocturnal creature
his eyes burn into me
becoming me
becoming the falcon circling
the bees droning in meadows of wild flowers
the children's voices
as they pluck blackberries
from the brambles

becoming the lanes of magnolia
between fading tangerine roses and purple irises
becoming my poems
my inky letters fading
words and stories fragile
on papers slightly yellowed

in a few months they will dream themselves
reborn into the heart of an arbutus tree
spreading roots in beds of coastal rock
in rainforests near the clay cliffs

and I have the wind and sea
in my voice
I harness the crescent moon
dragging it through unfurrowed fields
whispering a ragged prayer
to heron-priested skies.

The Body of My Garden

I have always
wanted words;
they bring me clarity,
reason, shape.

But my lover
paints, wordless
and love becomes
an art that preserves me,
time pouring out of rainforests,
rivers forming veins in my throat,
my limbs and bones and joints
and heart
in colours
spilling from brush
onto canvas.

The paints dream wet
verdant, ripening gardens of
magnolias, waxy pods
blooming into full fruit,
pools brimming with water lilies
and lotus.

Against a wide sky,
I am embedded in the mouths
of orchids,
in their nectaries,
tracing the delicate calyx
creamy petals,
hues of pale gold,
sap green.

In this language of the eye
this fierce gift of passion,
I am raw
words peeled away,
my skin oiled
with impasto layers,
thick flashes of
alizarin crimson
joy.

Belladonna

She reminds him to be vigilant
reminds him of the deadly nightshade
that threatens to overtake the garden

belladonna, beautiful lady
flowers such a deep lush purple
centers brilliant yellow
berries glisten so red

you want to taste one
but you know
it would stop your heart

Song of

I am a garden. Beyond my mazes and trellises are the whispers of winds, centuries of secrets. I offer you gifts. My gates are meant to be opened. Unfasten my latches.

I am the new day beginning, the time of singing. I am the voices of doves, the songs of many-mouthed birds. I am the sunlight streaming through your shuttered windows.

I am your cries. I am the wild, discordant call of herons.
I am the nocturnal hunter, the flight of hawks.

I am the kiss of winds. In my breath are spices for your mouth.

I am the resurrection
of found objects, of dust and peeling paint,
terraces of driftwood skeletons
salvaged from the sea.

I am the moss, the leaves, the grass.
I am our bed of green.

I am the blooming of flowers,
the purple embrace of clematis
bursts of ruby, ivory, saffron,
the perfumes of lilies, jasmine,
damask roses.

Come to me hungry and I will feed you.
I will give you the comfort of apples.
I am the taste of cherry, the tartness of lemons and oranges.
I am armfuls of plums and berries, sweet juices dripping down your throat.

Come to me thirsty and I will quench you.

I am the hummingbird
deep-plunged into fuschia blooms,
drinking nectar.
I will save this honey under my tongue
for you.

I am the beating of your heart
in the thrumming of my wings

I am the dragonfly
hovering
scarlet jewel
in amber air

I am wilderness
the secret places of cliff
the clefts of rock.
My branches and thorns
will catch you in their tangle.

I am your home.
I will house you
in the roof of my mouth
with pillars of smoke
and the fragrance of beams of cedar,
rafters of fir.

I am the flow of waters
of fountains and rivers and streams
of rains cleansing you
offering salve for your skin.

I am a wall
an enclosure
the keeper of vineyards and fortresses.
Unlock my silver fittings.

I am the day fading
the going down into flame
and sapphire
I am the shadow of your desire
dark and lovely
my hand plunged to the wrist into your grave.

I am the moon
fly my banners.

I am the earth
your companion.
I will hold you in the bowl of my hands
flesh warm and tender
rooting you in the rising of a new day.

I am the sun
seeded in you.

I am a garden.
Dwell in me.

Inhabited Heart

She drinks dark water
burns the blood
like powdered glass
rejecting
the geometry
she has learned.

Feels her way
into a lover's embrace,
water scalding,
leaping up into empty places
until her heart is filled with light
and infinite perfumes,
flesh of infants,
green of spring

the scent of blood
beating hard in the wrists
of arms that hold her

dancing
in cathedrals of the wind.

Autograph

your translations
of me
I could never
have anticipated

sheaves of my history
torn off by your glance

I am the blue-veined iris
in your hand
your fingers
dipped in me

I am signed by you
your name stroked
upon my forehead

Wild Poppy

The beach stretches before us,
grey with mud and wreckage washed up
by stormwinds, the sky cacophonous
with raucous gulls echoing our torn voices
the scarring torque of our words.

We are careful not to touch
no accidental brushing of skin.

But you cannot resist calling me over
to see, in the midst of wild grasses
an enormous bloom, swollen, surreal,
as if transplanted from some magical realm,

mystical planting of sweet, pink,

the poppy's petals enfold us,

its black and purple stained core
pulsing life into our chilled flesh.

Epithalamion

lifting high the garland gala roses white lilies
SHARON THESEN, "GALA ROSES"

She stands clothed
in the language of marriage,
shimmered silk,
orchids in her black hair
as they are double-ringed
in gold, banded
by ceremony.

They emerge
through kisses to sunbeams,
air fragrant with showers
of rose-petals,
blinding them.
Later, twirling
on the hook of him
across the dance floor
the grip of panic tightens
bent-iron in her throat.
She tosses
the clutch of roses and orchids
ribbons streaming across
a sea of virgins,
uplifted hands.
And she spins into his arms
the world's illusions
stains of form
flowing
lover to lover.

Hunger

When I realized
you never noticed
or felt joy
at the accidental beauty of things
I knew that to love you
above all others
is to know despair

memory insists
even in darkness
my fingers reading braille
the geography of your face, your body

you swallow me whole
never learning
to speak the language of my skin

the terrain of marriage
leaves me starving
mouth full of love.

Correspondence

The poem is not a cute
thing. Wearing the "manteau de voyage."
ERIN MOURÉ

I am missing you. The foghorns are moaning across the bay, shiplights gleaming near the point. I am reading women's lives, diaries rustling with muslins and silks, handwriting rippling across thick sheaves of paper. Their spines crack open, the long nerves of history exposed, threaded through me like the veins of your body.

Tonight I have your absence, the volumes of poetry you gave me, the red velvet of wine, my library of books. I want to run my hands along the lengths of shelves, finding places only you can read.

I am seeking a talisman, some charm for this journey. Perhaps the tiny bird bones you found on the beach, bleached skeleton and wings, ribs still attached to the spinal column—such a delicate ivory. Perhaps if I fasten them around my neck on a chain they will become my armour, so that only the pure of heart may enter.

In this hawk-eyed dusk, I am missing you. I am lighting candles in the rooms of my house. I have heard this is an act of faith. I am writing poems, my ragged prayers, these hauntings that beckon me with bony fingers through doors left ajar.

In the lunge of night, love unbolts the dark. The heart is a door, its hinges creaking open. I imagine the scent of my voice lives in you, under the skin of the ink-dark moon. I am dreaming you, the enigmas housed in your body, rain on your tongue, the weight of your hipbone, beloved wing writing letters of our being in the air, writing us into the eye of morning.

Gardens of Paradise:

Poems for Nur Jahan

From the legends of the paradise gardens, the harems and court life of the Mughal Empire, and from the tales of Empress Nur Jahan. The Empress was first called Nur Mahal, Light of the Palace, by her husband Emperor Jahangir, who selected her from his harem and married her in 1611. In 1616, she was given the title Nur Jahan, meaning Light of the World. Nur Jahan was a patron of the arts, a poet and a passionate designer of gardens. Like most of the women of the court, she wrote under the name of makhfi, "the concealed one," in reference to her life behind the palace (mahal) walls.

> *When I lift the veil from my face, a cry rises from the rose; if I put the comb to my tress, a moan comes forth from the hyacinth.*
>
> Nur Jahan

I

Chahar Bagh:
The Four Chambered Garden

She walks in garden paths,
symmetry veiled against the world

Beyond the walls, expanses of desert blazing
hot sands mapped by marauding strangers

Arid dreams loosen her, trembling
in enclosed chambers,

the pure spill of fountains, promises of Paradise

in the flesh of pomegranates

her silks rustle, anklets jingle,
aching to be the wind.

II

Dilkusha:
Garden of Heart's Delight

She walks in heart's delight
at Samarkand
composing ghazals

the morning opens blossoms
paths of white poplars
to the Turquoise Gates

In blue pools
his love turns her body
into water
eye-paint dripping into
foam

The key to her spirit
lies in his laughing mouth
masks discarded in fragrant jasmine
the scent of a king
in her black hair.

III

Kashmir

...mead after mead of flowers. Sweet -smelling plants
of narcissus, violet and strange flowers. The flowers of
Kashmir are beyond counting.

EMPEROR JAHANGIR

Wraps her
in his beloved Kashmir
in shawls of spring
embroidered with bindings
of tulips, almonds, peaches,
lilies and jasmine

preserves her in the brilliance
of scarlet roses
and the taste of sweet mangos.

IV

Dancing Girls

Music floats
beyond the palace walls
in the orchid sunset
the village girls
dream of silks and jewels
parties on trefoiled lawns

princesses of dust toil
pans of sand lifted on their heads
they become dancing girls
racing the wind
as they whirl their brooms
through the gutters

other days
they braid marigolds
in their hair
dance for men in the streets
filling their brothers' pockets
with rupees.

V

Vernag

In the pavilion
surrounded by colonnades
the Empress feeds him
mangoes and guavas
ripe figs from the orchards

lamps in brick cornices
glow on pools of fish
mead after mead of narcissus
groves of cypress

she commands the servants
as dancers and musicians
prepare for the feast

under the bitter orange trees
Nur Jahan remembers
her old geography

deep in a labyrinth
the harem thrives
she knows
the clink of gold bangles
a maze of women
labouring
to please their king
in nights of iris blue
stars trapped in shards
of mirrored hallways.

VI

The White Garden: Palace at Herat

The Joy House gardens
bloom cream and ivory
around a maze of rooms
labyrinths of women
where the emperor
keeps his secret treasure;
vish kanya she is called
she sips poison day by day
until her kiss
has the venom
of a cobra

the *vish kanya*, the king's gift
for those most deserving
bestowed on the friend
who betrays,
the enemy
to be entertained

during the festivities they are
lead by his eunuchs
to her chambers

drawn in by the lithe
innocence of her body
chambili, white jasmine behind her ear

the mercy of light
breaking open the sky
cannot save them

love becomes final
a deadly trick.

VII

Bagh-I Vafa:
Garden of Fidelity

Today he hunts tigers;
the sport reserved for kings
takes pleasure in the ceremony
of the kill

outside her skin
his pulse is beating

rubies at her throat
bleed rumours
through palace walls
seeping into
plots of imperial lilies.

in his chambers
bedclothes encrusted
with silver and gold
brocade loomed by beggars
smother her.

she joins the ghosts of other women
takes each reflection with her,
checks the glass for imperfections
kohl-rimmed eyes watching

the weight of him,
diamond-studded,
gold and heat burning
into her flesh.

VIII

Another Garden:
The Seeds of Empire

somewhere
away from his chambers
an infant girl is born
his unnamed flesh

whisked away to other gardens
embalms her cold-lipped
in marble fountains

harem mothers dream of sons
hearts steeled against
the tiny fists
hammering in their brains.

Child
of Our
Time

> Child
> of our time, our times have robbed your cradle.
> Sleep in a world your final sleep has woken
>
> EAVAN BOLAND,
> "CHILD OF OUR TIME"

> I believe I heard language through my mother's
> belly   both violent and sweet
>
> ROBIN BLASER,
> "STOP"

Copper Moon

For Matthew Shepard (1976-1998)
and for his mother and father, Judy and Dennis Shepard

>   *Child*
> *of our time, our times have robbed your cradle.*
> *Sleep in a world your final sleep has woken.*
>   EAVAN BOLAND, "CHILD OF OUR TIME"

In the wake of a thousand years,
your body a scarecrow
battered silhouette against the starlight
of a grave sky
death arrives in a pick-up truck
steals your shoes and $20 for coke and cigarettes
wraps your wallet in a dirty diaper
in a garbage pail
for this and for love
you are lashed to your crucifix
your blood a bitter stain
on the place that cradled you

your face
a scarlet mask
but for the clean white tracks
of your tears

and the air around us is a knife
and the taste of death is like rust
in our mouths
and a hundred years closes
a savage end to your journey

What hope for a new century
unless your brief shining will be
an ecclesiastes
unless in this broken place
some aurora of promise is born
unless your tears cleanse
the skin of the earth
unless our children,
born of this time and the next
learn from your severed wings
and fly
follow you out of this geography
this darkest heart

I imagine you there
in the primal glow
of a copper moon
the earth curving its shadow
across the lunar surface

There will be a season for you
when the trees and air and sky are singing
and light will begin in the roses opening,
in the apples falling from trees

and there will be a time for you
when the crows will disappear
mourning doves will vanish,
when faith will rise up
with the songbirds of dawn

May your breath be resurrected
by the human cantos of mercy.
May you dance beyond these years,
your heart breaking loose
in cathedrals of winds.

May this new century
hold you,
tender as a fontanel.

ii

You, Mr. McKinney, with your friend Mr. Henderson, killed my son....
You left him out there by himself, but he wasn't alone... he had the
beautiful night sky with the same stars and moon that we used to look
at through a telescope. Then he had the daylight and the sun to shine
on him one more time—one more cool, wonderful day in Wyoming.
His last day in Wyoming. And through it all he was breathing in for
the last time the smell of sagebrush and the scent of pine trees from the
snowy range. He heard the wind—the ever-present Wyoming wind—for
the last time.

DENNIS SHEPARD'S STATEMENTS TO THE COURT,
NOVEMBER 4, 1999

In the wake of a thousand years
I drift back on the bent neck of time
to the infant clasp of my firstborn
nursing her on an autumn night
her eyes reflecting
the milky net of stars

the earth curves its shadow
across the lunar surface
a copper moon glows over the foothills

and in this primal light
I give her to the tidal pulls of sleep and dreams,
my hand cupped beneath her heart

I remember her flight
through my cave of bones
her life spreading open
the beginning of music and light
an aperture of hope

in the folds of clean white linen
my child so new
all around her lightens and rises
claims me
the distillation of her breath
a universe,
an infinite refrain that enters me

iii

Baby boy

If anything stood out, it was the fragileness of Shepard
FIRESIDE LOUNGE EMPLOYEES CITED
BY PROSECUTOR CAL RERUCHA

Outside your funeral at the Redemption Chapel
Reverend Phelps marches
with his cronies from Kansas
their signs *God Hates Fags*
a full-color image of you says
Matthew in Hell

and it is a time to mourn
and a time to weep
a time to remember your father
teaching you songs of childhood
Frère Jacques,
Row, Row, Row Your Boat
Twinkle, Twinkle Little Star
how I wonder what you are
up above the world so high
like a diamond in the sky

the hatemongers at the temple
are surrounded
a parade of people dressed as "Angels of Peace"
white angels for you
seven feet high with eight foot wingspans
and the crowd cheers them on

I remember
that October night
at the Fireside Lounge,
how death courted you
beer bottle and pool cue in hand
discussing your politics
wrapping the syllables
of a serpent's coil
around your open heart
your smile shining
like your patent leather shoes

iv

this was someone's child
        MELISSA ETHRIDGE, "SCARECROW"

and I remember
another mother's voice
in a Laramie, Wyoming courtroom
claiming mercy for the murderers of her firstborn
Matthew stood for something
mercy for those who could not show mercy
and a father speaks to his son's killers:
I give you life in the memory
of one who no longer lives.
May you have a long life,
and may you thank Matthew
every day for it.
and I want the sanctity of scriptures
to conjure spells upon my tongue
to pray that this season too shall pass
as if the words might chant
a new scene into being

perhaps those farm fields
filled with wildflowers
the choirs of weeping
hushed in the opiate of poppies

but I see your pistol-whipped body
blood seeping into a nation
I remember the officer who cut you free
speaking of the braces on your teeth,
your school ID in the dust
she whispers to you in the ambulance
words of comfort, *Baby boy*
and the sound of mothers and fathers
through endless years
is a wailing of sirens in my ear

and I wonder, as I touch
the memory of my sleeping child
her tender fontanel,
as I watch her now
running fleet-footed
through corridors of time,
my anthem, my bloodline calling,
I wonder, if I could cast away stones,
if I could be so merciful
to those who would crush her

I wonder, if this new century
will hold her,
will her mother's faith in
memory's insistence,
be enough
for a millennium of mercy

Slippage

Now I see at the boundary of darkness
extreme of moonlight.

Stories From Boundary Bay

The road winds
a black ribbon
through the sky,
herons and cranes gracing
fields of grasses,
hawks on fenceposts
as I return to Boundary Bay
to the open arms of the sea
to the smell of kelp and ocean mists

I arrive home
weighed down
with briefcase and groceries
stacks of term papers
to grade
My students write about Romeo and Juliet
blur distinctions between text and film
Clare Danes and Leonardo DiCaprio
new heroes
to make their hormones surge
Shakespeare has never been so sexy
proclaim the slogans on posters
homage plastered on walls of
teenage girls' rooms

The Boundary Bay girls,
my daughter Rachel
KaseyBrookeSaraHaley their names inseparable
multisyllabic, all for one
the phone rings incessantly
They are playing
in the front yard
petals strewn across the pathway

Haley in a veil of white sheeting
another the groom, the taller one
enactments of the marriage script

Sometimes they do funerals

Daughters of feminists
spend hours
in front of mirrors
agonize about hair and nails
they pore collectively
over *Teen* and *Seventeen* magazines
wearing Tommy Girl and fragrances from The Gap
Grass, Earth, Dream, Heaven

Letter from Colleen
her mother died of cancer.
Years ago
LorrieColleenDebbie and I
spent summers reading Seventeen magazines
on hot days by the
Beaconsfield Swimming Pool

I see Colleen's mother finishing
the pale yellow hem
of her daughter's prom dress,
pins in her mouth
tenderly, tenderly
touches the corsage on her wrist
Today in Boundary Bay
the young girls gather
fluttering moths
to watch Brooke's older sister Nadine
prepare for the graduation dance

She is beautiful, glowing sleek
a slip of a dress-deep violet
hair upswept
the breathless waiting
for a young boy to pick her up
corsage her
time stands still
in the amber air of summer
such a bathing of expectancy
luminous promise
with its burden of radiance

And all around us
marriages fail
middle aged men leave their wives
for younger women
middle aged wives take lovers
or find basement apartments
Haley's mom left her second husband while he was out fishing,
Rachel tells me

In the unrest of passion, the disordered lyrics of love
paralysis and fear threaten to choke
the neighbourhood houses
at night the sounds of the sea, the tidal winds
mingle with the mooing of cows in farmers fields,
raccoons scavenging, stealing goldfish in backyard ponds,
coyotes howling in the woods

And in our gardens
pampas grasses whisper
they release a continuum
of repeated narratives
stories trapped in women's mouths

We lift each other up
when our knees buckle
underneath us
our children's needs
relentless magnets
anchoring us to the earth

I sit by the window
watching the night sky
the mother writing poems of girls
the art on white sheets like love
this one will be strong and fierce
this one will be tender and she will sing
shaping angels, prophets for the world
such terrifying beauty

In the gaps between my words
my daughters and their girlfriends slip
trying out to be cheerleaders
painting their fingernails blue and green
dreaming of bouquets from lovers
romancing the script

Slippage

My neighbor's house stands tall, exemplary,
a white standard on the tree-lined street where
spills of children play in the fragrance of
newly mown grass and friends gather like moths at
patio barbecues, swim laps in blue pools of suburbia.

Behind the pristine door
the air is scented with peach
and lemon pot-pourri,
imported soaps, Gucci colognes and
white terry cloth robes.

One night in June the cul-de-sac is lit up
red and blue lights pulsing in Delta Police cars

He is escorted from his home, the marriage ended
in restraint and order, his throat caught in the
noose of love.
His raging words burn a path
through his son's small body, across their lawn,
through his wife's rose bushes,

That night I dream of masked raccoons
night marauders, owls following the paths of headlights
a falcon circling small prey,
the tattered beat of wing.

I dream of consumption plants,
the choke of deadly nightshade, stinging nettles along
the Serpentine River

I dream a black fisted storm, a singular fury,
lightning razoring the neighbor's pine tree,
its scent in my nostrils crashing through my roof.

In the morning,
the tree still stands outside my window.
The sun rises, a warm peach offering up
seaside angelica, the air full of anise swallowtails and
red admiral butterflies.

At dawn,
I slip into my daughters' rooms and listen
to their measured breaths,
stroke their hair softly back from their foreheads.

If the Heart Asks For Pleasure First

My daughter emerges from
the pastel cocoon
of her room
through the ticking
of the hallway clock
floats down the stairs
into the dusk
as the stream of possible lovers begins

I still imagine her slender bones
need cradling
her body light as a dragonfly
skeletal recesses like a soft-shelled crab
an easy mark
for crushing

her face mine, ours
the tendrils of youth
still visible
her separateness a gift
tied with the full weight
of my heart-salt

as she enters the night sky
orchid and indigo
the evening news tells stories
of clipped wings, small coffins
the earth scarred with grief
hearts opened and closed

and I am reminded of what I know
that there is nothing stronger
than to be helpless before desire
knowing that moment when

the heart must answer yes
when there is no longer
any choice but assent

tonight at my desk
covered with papers
scraps of poems
every alphabet my child
my heart stops and starts in the dark
until the sound of her key in the lock
my necessary lullaby

Valentine

Most days I am content
having folded away the blueprints
of another life
but it is February, a restless dusk.
Our daughter cuts out
paper hearts at the kitchen table
Valentines for classmates
Be Mine, My One and Only,
Mi Corazon, Heart's Desire
snip, snipping
pink and red ribbons
drifting to the floor.

Vancouver rain soaks the windowpanes
steel guitar strings strumming love songs
on the bay obscured by mists.

If I listen long enough
I'll no longer yearn for your voice
I'll lose myself in whispers
from the ivy covered walls
of the Sylvia Hotel.
The lovers' trysts will warm me,
take me into their stories for awhile.

A lifetime ago
I used to cut roses and peonies from the garden
gathering perfume from the evening sky
arranging them in blown glass
petals drifting onto
the grooved oak of our dining table
their fragrance sweet against the steam
of roast chicken, wild asparagus
new potatoes and garlic.

My eyes turn grey.
I break in the waves
of a west coast storm
longing for candied hearts, cinnamon spiced,
for the days and nights
of stealing poetry from the air,
for your arms full of flowers,
your shoes, shiny
step, stepping
through our front door.

Birthday Poem For Rachel

I want to whisper you awake
this morning
your body warm in a nest of sleep

the sky is a smile of light
the sun's breath rising,
writing the lyrics of your limbs
into the still waters of the bay

water birds are calling your name
steeple stemmed herons ankle the wetlands
white cranes stilt across the mudflats

scarlet poppies seed themselves
in wild grasses for you

seaweed glistens,
wraps the beach with
streamers of emerald ribbons

Child, you are my hymn
my anthem
my bloodline calling

I wish you gifts:
to feel along the heart
to sense with the pulse
to find the light that breaks
through secret places
unbolting the dark

to dance fleet-footed
through corridors of dreams

on your year's turning
may you find the map of love
charted in these shores
whispered in winds
and in the sleek mouths of seals.

Catherine

for Catherine Jane Troy Dunlop (1926-1997)

The Ship's Company of the "Aquitania" send you best wishes
for your happiness and good fortune in your new life in the
great Dominion, the country of your adoption.
                                        MARCH 1946

Widow's skin parched
spilling memory in waves
bloodremembering
across cool, hospital sheets.

Dreams of dancing
her gnarled joints unknotted,
flesh supple,
spinning to Tommy Dorsey's big band music
cheek held against his khaki uniform
his wide smile spanning
the smoke-filled canteen.

She remembers scents,
liquid memories, exotic promise
in the drabness of war
Crepe de Chine, Shalimar
In London at the chemist's shop
her soldier buys her Chanel No.5.

The chemist has a nose for perfume
The top note, he tells them, the one you smell first,
is the man-made synthetic aldehyde
then the middle notes, jasmine, lily of the valley, orris-root and ylang-ylang.
Finally, the base notes that make the perfume linger:
vetiver, sandalwood, cedar, vanilla, amber, civet and musk.
Base notes are of animal origin, ancient memories of smell beginning
in vast plains and forests.

It is scent that disturbs her drift of sleep
perfumare, through smoke.

She remembers ships of war brides
with their infants cradled
in the scent of salt air,
sailing into the arms
of Halifax harbour.

She becomes his geography
inhabited by mists,
Atlantic foam at her feet,
her body embedded
in fields of violets and wild berries,
endless harvests,
her blood flowing
in the veins
of a new country.

Now, she resists the pull
of winter,
the deep white territory
of skin and ghosts

she insists upon another day
does not want the slow descent
into ice.

I reach for her to stop time
with my heat
breathing fire into
the clasp
of paper dry hands.

Variations of Blue:
Foreign Correspondence

i

My task was to prove that the origin of language was the desire to
express colour;...I saw only blue, the air, the land, the sea—all were
blue. Through a blue glass, where the glass was ubiquitous.

RICHARD LANE, "FOUND OBJECT—HORNBY ISLAND,"
VANCOUVER NOTEBOOKS

I read your letters in my garden
fragrant with lavender and hyacinth,
blooming with periwinkle and blue Himalayan poppies

You write to me often about the colour blue

blue is between us
our letters and e-mails exhaled through winds
rippling waters like blown ink,
skies quarrying turquoise and ultramarine

I send you poems invoking pillow books of
tenth century Japanese courtesans
writing on scrolls of indigo paper, wrapping lovers in
indigo silk

blue soaks the spaces between our words
in the twilight hour, *l'heure bleue*

your letters reach me in cobalt dusks
your English Channel and rivers and lakes
veining their cartography like irises under my skin

alchemy begins in the blue vault of memories
you write Vancouver, *a cool blue burning of place*

your soul hallucinates coastal landscapes
Japanese mists float and filter through
days of deep shades of blue, Picasso blue, blue mountains
                    snow on the North Shore summits a hint
        of ice-blue
the blue silk stretch of Boundary Bay

on dark nights your letters soften in my hands
I hold words in my arms like lilac branches
gathered from the perfumed air

ii

the round key to the universe, which is so quick;
come touch the fire of this momentary blue,
before its petals wither.

PABLO NERUDA, SONNET XXIV

we have been tentative, proper,
with our correspondences,
achieving the right distance

but things fall apart at the centre
past lives flounder and drown
bruised histories collide in strange synchronicity
hearts brushed blue with cold
bodies turning on beds of stone

we write as if our words might contain some magic
written into the air like spells and incantations

I write to you as if my syllables could heal,
my calligraphy a blue salve,
an infusion of cool waters for the heart's desert

our letters become surprises
gifts like the flash of a heron's wing
old dreams closing in nocturnal air
new dreams opening the moon in verse
our language a punctuation of flesh and bone
in the breath of tides

We do not see each other often
passing in flight, airports and foreign cities
your visits to Vancouver,
but when you write about that painting in London

at the Whitechapel Gallery
a rare cubist canvas stroked with
such intense variations of living, pulsing shades of blue
it made you weep

when you write of this blue intensity of tears
I know that such a response to blue
will survive the passing of the years,
the crumbling of bones, our distances and silences

such a response to blue
wraps a lyric shawl about my throat,
close to the pulse of my blood
I will always know your absence
as an alphabet; it spells my name.

49 Degrees North
and Beyond

Here, everything is named for orchard country:
Cherry Lane, Peachland, Summerland.
Over the seasons I learn the grammar and syntax of fruit,
in a place where Bartlett pears waltz from trees
and cherry blossoms intoxicate with fragrant spills of blooms,
where the scent of Ponderosa pines fills the air,
their branches reaching across a salmon dusk.

Now, along Naramata Road,
the grapes are being harvested,
ripening on the vines and bursting
into winemakers' Reislings and champagnes
and the sweet ferment of ice wines.

And this valley with its lush, verdant heart,
crackles with dry, desert heat,
tumbleweed blowing across the highway.

We came here hungry
our mouths finding each other
in seasons of plums
but it is a dry season now
with the threat of frost
and it is only on fevered nights
of blood-rememberings
that I recall the taste of fruit
on your lips.

Strange moon suspended
in daylight over the lake.
We want things as they were,
the long nights

punctured by stars
the sun bursting open
dawn delirious
on our skins.

Concordance

The air is a knife
the sharp intake of winter
frost over Ladner farms
a Diebenkorn landscape
and the sky full of thunder
the beat of wings
hawks, kestrels, geese, starlings
thousand of birds
on the Pacific Flyway.

The continent is heaving
with the drumming of flight
to Asia and Africa
and South America

my heart skips a beat, shifts

a lone crane spreads its wings
hesitates
and decides to stay.

This
Tender
Music

Music arrives, searching for us. What hope or memory without it.
Whatever we may think. After so many words.

The music's pirated from somewhere else: Catalan songs reaching us
after fifty years. Old nuevos canciones, after twenty years? In them,
something about the sweetness of life, the memory of traditions of
mercy, struggles for justice. A long throat, casting memory forward.

ADRIENNE RICH,
"A LONG CONVERSATION"

The Garden of My Familiar

We exist, given the presence of our familiars.
LOUISE BOGAN

The day opens
waking us to songs
multitudes of red-throated birds
sunlight streams through
shuttered windows

In the garden
the terrace spills
blooms lush against
driftwood
salvage from the beach
bursts of pinks and corals
purple embrace of clematis
and wild plum trees

a hummingbird drinks nectar
from the belled tongues
of fuschia

a scarlet bird hovers
jewel-like
in amber air

I hear the beat of your heart
in the thrumming
of its wings

my daughter Rachel
presses wildflowers
on a page of poems
gifts she writes for me

as day slips into indigo
the garden holds us
in the bowl of her hands
flesh warm and tender
rooting us
in a blue-heron sky.

Prelude

You and I in a garnet spill
of sun plunging into
cherry orchards.
We learn to dance to
open tunings of flaming violins.

I inhale hyacinths upon your wrists.

In the ink swell of night
darkness in the still throat of water
we drink tea and brandy
through the strains
of opera.

The scent of you is there,
laced through the bones
of the moon
in silver infusions
of stars and Mozart

and I slip liquid
from my skin
into the sweet,
soft taste of dusk.

Canto

Real singing is a different movement of air.
Air moving around nothing. A breathing in a god. A wind.
RAINIER MARIA RILKE

Let me be your real singing in this world, a canto heavy with hunger that spills my notes into the opened muscles of your heart. Let me be your piano player, my fine-toothed keys tapping code, an enigmatic, secret music. Let me be your cracked code, your canary song.

Let me be your beloved choir, a chant, a chorus of wings. Let this singing be a breathing of oceans and the steady rhythms of the wings of sea birds.

Let this be your song, a poem to take in your mouth, taste the words on your tongue. These will be the disordered lyrics of love. They will be hot, red siren notes, quickening the pulse. They will be cool, blue riffs, liquid vibrations in your throat.

Let me be the sound that opens your body into weightlessness, an aria lifting you into the scald of moonlight, a crescendo of stars.

Let me fill you with the inner music of roses, their fragrant prayers. Let me be your aubade, the song you hear in the opening hours of each day, your matins, octaves of light rising. Let me be your evening vespers, your nocturne in the flames going down. Let me be your lulla-by, your soprano wind, my phrasings and stanzas holding you in the grace of a slow tender music.

Let me be the ballad that binds you to the earth, that mourns, that peels away your skin, clasps your bones. Let me be a song to die in.

Let me be your psalm of faith, your sacred vernacular, so that we may not be broken by the world's darkness.

Scordatura

Vancouver, January 31, 1998

The posturing glitterati
at the art gallery
chatter in front of Edvard Munch's sick children
suffering men and women
agonized souls.

The air becomes cloying;
we escape gasping
into the night.

In Duthie's Books we browse
through new releases
bell hooks'
The Wounds of Passion: A Writing Life.
I am drawn to it
wanting words for my poet self
but the cover image burns
hands scored with stigmata
patio, the root of passion,
meaning suffering.

We step back into the street
through the crush of people
to find a busker
fingerless gloves plucking beauty
on a bandura
the strains of Pachelbel's Canon
are made new
his hands opening harp strings
into the air.

The night stills,
through time's disordered architecture
spilling over history's fragile dams
as I remember meeting you
in the brink of my soul's winter
when you gave me the smoke of your breath
in the long night
the stars emptying such clear light
in you
such clear light
love's sonata carving music
across the sky.

Night Flight: Winter Solstice

On the eve of a performance of the Yarker Chamber Music Society
THE OLD SCHOOLHOUSE, YARKER,
ONTARIO, DEC. 16, 2000

On this night
the sun melts a scarlet fire
into the violet and indigo
of the night sky.
On this night they say
the sun will return at midnight
and the dark hours will lift
across the trees.

At the Old Schoolhouse
the Chamber musicians prepare for performances,
their open tunings, the discordant keenings
of instruments.

The words "chamber music" echo hollow
through my discarded memories,
an abacus spills through my hair
burnt cinders fly from my mouth.

I drift along the edges of time
and I am a small girl in Montréal,
my velvet jumper,
my long black braids tied with ribbons,
my patent leather shoes,
in the church hall
the music solemn, mournful,
the notes held
in my mother's rigid backbone,
her stern spine pinning me into proper place.

But tonight the moon unwinds her blue,
blesses the babies and friends who gather,
Gary and Rena, little Hayden in his
red flannel shirt, newborn Zinta, her angel breath.

And the concert begins,
Rena's hands flying over the piano,
James on the flute.
The air weeps.

Tonight my long black hair
is unbound.
Dressed in my velvet
I think of you
my heart loosened in a *Pavane,*
cradled by a Fauré *Berceuse.*

Outside, the birds
begin their nocturnal flights
and tonight
in this roomful of people
I know we are all helpless
in the face of love
fragile as the inner flesh of
a bare wrist.

In this night music,
in the symphony of wingbeats,
the heart lightens and rises.

Nocturne

I

We are changed by the earth's music
not the contained notations
but the scores that sing
the randomness of moonlight
and birth and death
the notes of our daily vernacular
concerts in the kneading of bread
of the mother rocking her infant
the ecstatic passages of making love
the sounds of a Gregorian chant
your metronomed heart
skipping a beat.

II

Full moon
vernal equinox
swift eclipse
soft prayers in the forest
slow minor harmonies
the moan of hunger
against the strains
of nocturnal perfumes
played into
our cupped hands.

III

We have the same heat
you and I
your oils, my inks,
on primed canvasses and parchment sheets
we play each other
ascending scales of crimson
burning long chords of fire
in the blackened altars of the night.

Essential Gestures

She writes
sweet offerings,
confessionals of desire
moderato cantabile

and seeks to fill
the spaces of her body,
her echo chambers,
with the pulses
of more potent unguents

intertwining them,
enmeshed
in nets of words,
wet silks nuzzled
into the rough,
drawing the threads,
the open strings,
leaning out of Mozart,
dancing
on the chords of Bach
into the sacred winds
through the forests
of Racine,
folding, unfolding
the fresh, white sheets
in the symphonic
clasp
of hands.

Gifts

The composition of desire
is always a mystery
nights disturbed
by old thirst and hungers
nerves exposed in preludes
to moonlight
hearts strung on the chords
of the wind
the arc of a melody
ascending my spine
in faint, impossible dreams.

The body's harmony bleeds
silenced in your absence
everything in me broken.

Still, I would give you
morning songs of violins,
night-blooming jasmine,
roses in my opened hands,
a Venetian goblet
full of shattered stars.

Grace in Another Landscape

To walk with you
chin deep
in purple coneflowers,
in wild poppies,
in candelabras of sunlight,
is to find another landscape,
foreign territory, yet familiar.

This earth sings
of what holds us fast
beyond sensibility,
the open strings of crickets,
the hum of bees
sounding us home.

The Fragrance of Love

Love has a particular scent.
This is not mythology. It is
a stirring of convulsive beauty.

I have inhaled this fragrance, tasted it
in blood in the silk of my newborn's hair,
in the wildsweet of my lover's eyes,

in the salt tongues of oceans,
in the quicksilver streams of
estuaries, in the damp smell of
honeysuckle, in the language of
midnight and storms and volcano
hearts, in the musk of autumn days,
crisp with scarlet and ochre,

in the white-pitched fever of the
evening moon, rising everywhere.

Most of all, I have found it
in that rosebush you saved from
demolition, your bleeding hands deep
in the earth, excavating and replanting
in my garden.

Today the roses bloom and bloom,
their perfume your lush and heady gift.
I will have this fragrance until flowers
open into infinity, and all that is
becomes stillness.

By this measure I am undone.
By this measure I have lived.

ACKNOWLEDGEMENTS

I would like to thank Joseph Paczuski for his belief in this manuscript and for directing it into the right hands. My heartfelt gratitude to Denis DeKlerck for his thoughtful editing and for bringing this book into print. My gratitude also to Pier Giorgio Di Cicco, for his mentorship, editing advice, and loving support of my work. My special thanks to Gailene Powell for her valued readings, critiques, and tireless support. Thanks to Karleen Pendleton Jimenez for her thoughtful responses to some of these poems. Thanks to Carl Leggo, Stephen Carey, Laurie Ricou, and Richard Lane for their support and readings. I would like to acknowledge my appreciation of Gabriel Caira for his beautiful cover design and to photographer Barbara Cole for her cover image.

The author gratefully acknowledges the following publications in which many of these poems were originally published: ARM, Summer 2002. "Slippage, " "Catherine." *Poiesis*, Spring 2002. "Eros," "Prayer." *ARM, Fall/Winter, 2001, Vol.3, No.2.* "Copper Moon." *Arm, Fall/Winter, 2001, Vol.3, No.2.* "The Garden of My Familiar;" "Prayer;" "Night Flight: Winter Solstice;" "Concordance." *Event: Spring 2000.* "If the Heart Asks for Pleasure First." *Dandelion, Spring 1999.* "Epithalamion." *Contemporary Verse 2 (CV2), Vol. 21, No.1, 1998.* "Stories From Boundary Bay" (First Prize Winner Poetry Contest). *Whetstone, Spring 1998.* "Slippage," earlier version titled "Happy Families." *JCT 1998.* "Essential Gestures." *Whetstone, Fall 1997.* "The Body of My Garden;" Gardens of Paradise: Poems for Nur Jahan: "Chahar Bagh: The Four Chambered Garden;" "Dilkusha: Garden of Heart's Delight;" "Kashmir;" "Another Garden: Seeds of Empire;" "Bagh-I-Vafa: Garden of Fidelity." The poems "Birthday Poem for Rachel" and "Stories From Boundary Bay" were performed in a Spoken Word performance for International Women's Day, March 8, 2001, at the National Arts Centre, Ottawa. The poems were published in a chapbook anthology of Canadian women poets titled *A Celebration of Women in the Arts*, Talking Marigold and mother tongue books. Poems in the sections The Body of My Garden and Slippage formed a manuscript that was a finalist for the CBC-Saturday Night Canada Council Award for Poetry in 1998. These poems were subsequently published as a chapbook titled *Boundary Bay*, by Staccato Chapbooks in 2000, distributed by Turnstone Press.

Notes

The poems in Perpetual Angelus: "Rush Hour at Bloor Station," "What the Heart Knows," and "Vespers" incorporate fragments from T.S. Eliot's "Burnt Norton," "East Coker," " The Dry Salvages," and "Little Gidding" in *Four Quartets*.

Rishma Dunlop is a professor of Literary Studies in the Faculty of Education, at York University, Toronto. She is a poet and fiction writer whose work has won awards and has appeared in numerous books, journals, and anthologies, nationally and internationally. She was a finalist for the 1998 CBC/Saturday Night Canada Council Literary Awards for poetry. Her novel, *Boundary Bay*, was a semi-finalist for the inaugural Chapters/Robertson Davies Prize in 1999. She is the author of a previous volume of poetry, *Boundary Bay*, published by Staccato Chapbooks (2000).